Full Throttle

PT Cruiser

Tracy Nelson Maurer

Rourke

Publishing LLC

Vero Beach, Florida 32964

www.rourkepublishing.com

PHOTO CREDITS: Page 4 (Orville Wright) Library of Congress; all other images courtesy DaimlerChrysler

Also, the author extends appreciation to Julie Lundgren, John Kari, Mike Maurer, Lois M. Nelson, and the team at Rourke Publishing.

Editor: Robert Stengard-Olliges
Page Design: Tara Raymo

Notice: The publisher recognizes that some words, model names, and designations mentioned herein are the property of the trademark holder. They are used for identification purposes only. This is not an official publication.

Library of Congress Cataloging-in-Publication Data

Maurer, Tracy, 1965-
  PT Cruiser / Tracy Nelson Maurer.
     p. cm. -- (Full throttle 2)
  Includes bibliographical references and index.
  ISBN 978-1-60044-576-7
  1. PT Cruiser automobile--Juvenile literature. I. Title.
  TL215.P8M38 2008
  629.222'2--dc22
                              2007014843

Printed in the USA

IG/IG

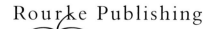

Rourke Publishing

www.rourkepublishing.com – rourke@rourkepublishing.com
Post Office Box 3328, Vero Beach, FL 32964

Table of Contents

Shaped by the Past

Today's **retro** car designs blend advanced technology with classic styling. A retro car often recalls a popular version in the model's past. Introduced in 2001, the first PT Cruiser drew inspiration from the historic—but mostly unpopular—1930s Chrysler Airflow. Style creativity from 1950s hot rods also showed in the early PT Cruiser design. Today, the PT Cruiser revs up the retro look with stylish upgrades and fun attitude.

In the late 1920s, Chrysler engineers studied how air flowed over objects at higher speeds—a science now known as **aerodynamics**. Chrysler tested its ideas in Orville Wright's **wind tunnel**—advanced technology in the 1920s for any carmaker.

Fast Fact

Orville and Wilbur Wright studied aerodynamics to build a flying machine in 1903.

*The Chrysler Airflow became America's first aerodynamic, full-size **production car**. The sleek car offered a smoother ride, tighter handling, greater speed, and better fuel economy than other family cars of its time.*

4

aerodynamics
   engineering designs that allow air to flow easily over the body for greater speed

production car
   the final model of a design, ready for manufacture

retro
   designed to recall something from the past, such as a car model

wind tunnel
   a tunnel where air blows at known speeds to test a car's aerodynamics

Airflow Innovations

- Seating within the two axles—an idea still used today
- Engine over the front wheels to balance weight front to back
- Lower stance than most American cars
- Sloped grille instead of upright radiator
- Headlights tucked near the grille
- "V"-shaped windshield to slice through the wind
- Strong, full steel body; not a wooden frame as most cars used then
- Fenders over the tires to direct airflow around the car
- Among the first American cars to hide the spare tire in the trunk

Chrysler made the Airflow only from 1934 to 1937. It sold poorly during the Great Depression. Americans had no money to risk on a new car design.

Hot Rod Heritage

After World War II ended in 1945, a lot of Americans traded in their 1930s cars for glitzy new models. Cheap old cars filled junkyards and dealership back lots. Creative mechanics fixed the "vintage tin" into fast street machines. These wild custom cars were called hot roadsters, or hot rods.

Hot rod fans called their unique vehicles rolling works of art. Hot rods often sported bright colors and painted flames. They had chopped, or lowered, roofs—or no roof at all. Hot rods also shook the street with powerful engines. Illegal street races gave hot rods a shady reputation.

The National Hot Rod Association started in 1951 to help move drag racing to the racetracks instead of the streets. It's one of the world's largest racing organizations today.

*Big carmakers mostly ignored hot rods. Then in 1993, Chrysler introduced the Prowler **concept car**. The bold retro body shape honored America's hot rod culture. Chrysler made about 11,700 Prowlers between 1997 and 2002.*

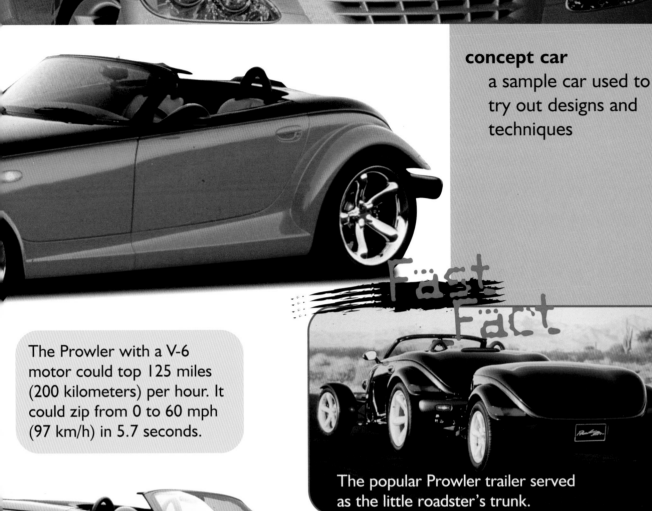

concept car
a sample car used to try out designs and techniques

The Prowler with a V-6 motor could top 125 miles (200 kilometers) per hour. It could zip from 0 to 60 mph (97 km/h) in 5.7 seconds.

Fast Fact

The popular Prowler trailer served as the little roadster's trunk.

Fast Fact

In 1999, Chrysler unveiled its Howler concept based on the Prowler. The new 250-horsepower "hot rod truck" proved people still liked the wild styling.

The 1997 Prowler came in Purple Metallic. That's it—no choices.

7

The Prowler and the Howler confirmed Chrysler's hunch that a whole bunch of buyers might like to drive an affordable hot rod. The company's designers borrowed the Prowler's bulging fenders, sloping grille, and low stance for a practical retro-styled compact car. In 1997, the Pronto concept car and the Chrysler CCV (Composite Concept Vehicle) prototype hinted at the company's newest idea for the streets.

Fast Fact

In 2000, the Museum of Modern Art in New York City displayed the Chrysler CCV for its unique design.

MOPAR®

Chrysler merged with Daimler-Benz in 1998 to become DaimlerChrysler. Car buffs call any car from Chrysler a "Mopar." Mopar comes from "Motor Parts," a 1930s Chrysler auto parts business still operating today.

When the Chrysler PT Cruiser hit showrooms in 2001, even its badge featured retro styling. Walter P. Chrysler first used a badge with silver wings and a golden seal when he started his car company in 1925. Today, all Chrysler cars use the classic badge.

Fast Fact

Chrysler's brands include Dodge and Jeep. The Plymouth brand closed in 2001.

Fast Fact

Chrysler engineer Fred Zeder worked on the Airflow and other innovative cars. Some people think the logo's tiny thunderbolts are "Z"s to honor him.

New Rules

Chrysler set new rules for compact cars when it launched the PT Cruiser in 2001. The rules said a little car could be practical, fun to drive, and still look hot. The PT Cruiser blended the size of a compact car with the loading style of a minivan and jazzed it up with retro Airflow styling. The PT Cruiser snagged big awards from the start:

- *Car and Driver* Ten Best for 2001
- North American Car of the Year 2001
- *Consumer Guide* Automotive Compact Car Best Buy 2001-2006 (six years in a row!)

In a way, the PT Cruiser looks like a mini minivan. The basic model has four doors and a rear gate that lifts open with hinges at the roof.

Chrysler said "PT" stands for Personal Transportation. Some fans think it also means "Plymouth Truck," a line of 1930s models.

The PT Cruiser comfortably seats five and holds luggage in the back. The vehicle measures about 169 inches (429 cm) from nose to tail. That's shorter than a Dodge Caliber or Dodge Neon.

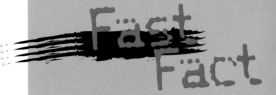
Fast Fact

The PT Cruiser seems big, but it fits into a compact parking space.

People have called the PT Cruiser a compact station wagon, a hatchback, and a mini minivan. They all mean the same low, boxy PT Cruiser shape. The shape has stayed the same since 2001. However, Chrysler has offered a range of PT Cruiser packages with a variety of **options**, such as leather seats or shiny 17-inch (43-cm) wheels. Some of the editions included Classic, Limited, Touring, Pacific Coast Highway, and GT.

MAJOR MODEL MILESTONES

YEAR	MODEL
1994-1998	Concept and prototype cars
2001	Introduced PT Cruiser
2003	Turbocharged GT model
2005	Convertible
2006	Style update for 2007

A special rear badge shows the edition name.

*The PT Cruiser Convertible measures slightly less than the **sedan** in length and height. The two styles share the same width and **wheelbase**.*

*In 2005, Chrysler cranked up the
fun factor on the PT Cruiser by introducing a convertible
option. It has two doors and seats four people.*

*The PT Cruiser uses a sport
bar at the middle to
strengthen the car's frame.
It adds rollover safety, too.
The sport bar also lifts
airflow above rear-seat
passengers. The ride is
less drafty and quieter
than typical convertibles.*

A special window treatment
helps reduce glare and cabin
heat on sunny days.

The PT Cruiser sold well from the start. Americans snapped up the friendly hot rod, sometimes paying more than the car's window sticker price. Generally, PT Cruisers cost around $20,000. The PT Cruiser quickly became popular around the world. Chrysler has sold PT Cruisers in more than 50 countries.

Workers can build a PT Cruiser in about 38 hours.

A factory in Toluca, Mexico, has built every PT Cruiser since the year 2000. The huge facility covers more than 1.5 million square feet (139,350 sq m). About 3,400 employees work at the plant.

The Toluca factory can build about 180,000 cars each year. In 2006, the plant built the 1,000,000th PT Cruiser.

The Retro Ride

The PT Cruiser uses retro styling outside and inside. The car's shape, borrowed from the Airflow and hot rods, sets the retro theme. Then smaller retro details add to the effect. These details don't always point back in time to a certain model. They just *feel* retro. The PT Cruiser also blends modern comfort, convenience, and safety into the unique compact package.

On the PT Cruiser, the outside metallic door handles accent the retro theme. Passengers must push the door button with their thumbs. Then they can pull the door open.

Updates for the 2007 PT Cruiser feature a scalloped effect for the double headlights. The unusual headlight shape shows a flair for design, much like hot rod cars do.

The PT Cruiser GT Edition comes with a rear spoiler in the same color as the body. The spoiler reduces lift and improves traction at higher speeds.

From behind, the PT Cruiser finishes the retro look with taillights shaped like teardrops. The lights swoop downward off the bulging rear fenders as if blown by a rushing wind.

The PT Cruiser's chrome accented grille still slopes from the high hood. It recalls the historic Airflow. The silver wing badge crowns the grille.

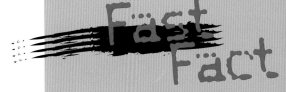

Retro styling continues inside the PT Cruiser. The winged badge appears in a few places, such as the middle of the steering wheel. Round gauges with chrome accents follow the theme, too. The "PT Cruiser" name also marks the dashboard. The name's font uses a retro effect that also suggests the car's hot rod heritage, in case anyone forgets.

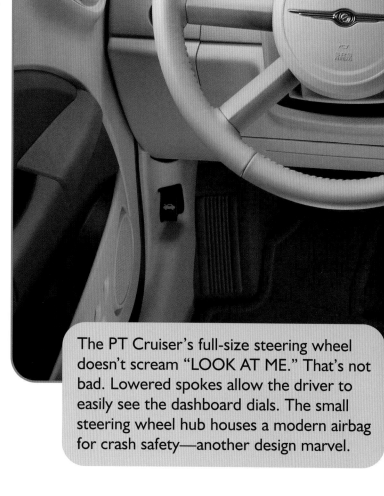

The interior instrument panel color matches the exterior color.

The PT Cruiser's full-size steering wheel doesn't scream "LOOK AT ME." That's not bad. Lowered spokes allow the driver to easily see the dashboard dials. The small steering wheel hub houses a modern airbag for crash safety—another design marvel.

analog clock
a clock with hands

Digital clocks light up the control panels of most cars on the road today—but not in the PT Cruiser. The designers chose an old-fashioned **analog clock** instead. The clock's center position in the dashboard reminds passengers that this is a retro ride.

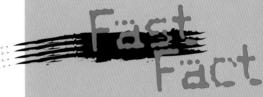

Window controls are mounted on the center console—just to look different.

Most PT Cruisers feature a handy electronic vehicle information center. The center shows the traveling direction, temperature, average fuel economy, and other important facts. An optional dash mounted electronic map is not available on the convertible.

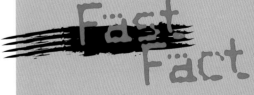

The retro shifter knob reminds many people of a cue ball.

Chrysler engineers plugged into computerized "virtual reality" and other **simulation** programs to experiment with creative ideas for the PT Cruiser. Online teamwork helped to build a surprisingly roomy and comfortable interior. The teamwork also produced some thoughtful features for the compact car.

Why stop with cool door handles on the outside? Interior teardrop shaped door handles accent the retro theme for passengers. The handles were first sculpted from balsa wood. Then the design was scanned into a computer for the team to see.

Fast Fact

The sedan's rear seats split 65/35, meaning one folding section is larger than the other. The convertible has a 50/50 split, meaning each half can fold.

The PT Cruiser makes up for its compact size by offering big choices inside the car. The rear seats and the front passenger seat fold flat. The rear seats also tumble forward or remove completely. In all, the car has 32 different seating arrangements.

simulation
an example or model of a certain situation used to test ideas and make improvements

The sport bar features built-in courtesy lamps—a first for any carmaker.

In the late 1990s, safety experts learned that static electricity from car seats could spark a fire at the fuel pump. The PT Cruiser has specially treated fabric on the seats to resist static and stains. It's still best to stay outside the car after starting to pump gasoline.

No one should reach or sit inside a vehicle after starting the fuel pump.

Practical Power

The showroom PT Cruiser looks revved up, but its power is more practical than race ready. Chrysler developed an inline four-cylinder engine. Each of the four cylinders, or combustion chambers, has four valves to control the mix of air and fuel. In the United States, the PT Cruiser offers only a 2.4-liter gasoline engine. A smaller 2.2-liter diesel engine has been available in Europe, Asia, and South Africa.

2.4L TURBO

PT Cruisers deliver fuel economy that ranges from 22 miles per gallon (9 kilometers per liter) for city driving to 29 mpg (12 km/l) for highway driving.

In 2003, Chrysler put more growl under the PT Cruiser's hood by adding a **turbocharger** option for the Limited and the GT editions. The High-Output (HO) GT turbocharger delivers 230 horsepower. That's almost double what a standard PT Cruiser engine can muster.

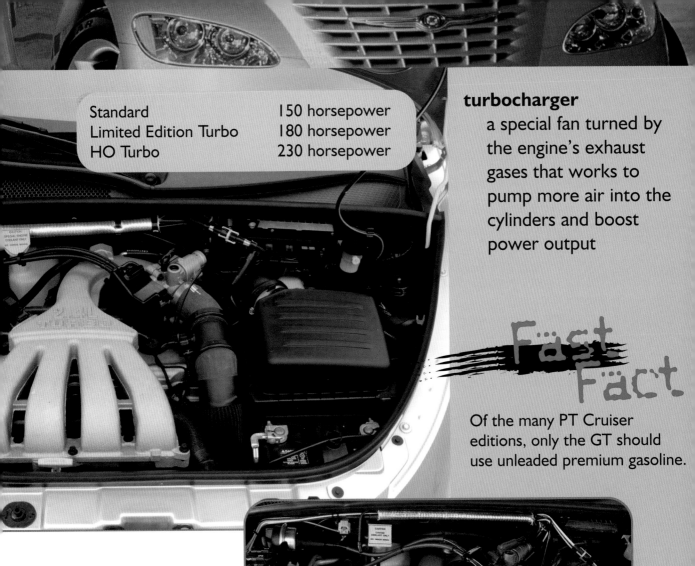

Standard	150 horsepower
Limited Edition Turbo	180 horsepower
HO Turbo	230 horsepower

turbocharger
a special fan turned by the engine's exhaust gases that works to pump more air into the cylinders and boost power output

Fast Fact

Of the many PT Cruiser editions, only the GT should use unleaded premium gasoline.

The HO turbocharger launches from 0 to 60 mph (97 km/h) in 6.8 seconds. It blasted a quarter mile (0.4 km) time of just over 15 seconds, too. Not supercar timing, but peppy for a compact car.

Under all the retro design work, advanced technology delivers the PT Cruiser's crisp handling. The stiff frame, **suspension**, and brakes work in harmony to respond to the driver's commands. The car tracks well even at higher speeds, keeping the tail aligned with the nose.

Turbo PT Cruisers feature a specially tuned suspension for a tighter, sportier ride. The engineers also roughed up the exhaust note for a more beastly sound.

The turbo PT Cruiser has a custom-inspired 2.75-inch diameter (7 cm) exhaust tip, touched with classy chrome.

suspension
in a vehicle, the system of shock absorbers, springs, and other parts between the wheel and frame designed to create a smooth ride and better control

The car beeps in reverse like construction vehicles. The PT Cruiser's safety alert helps drivers avoid trouble.

Fan Favorite

The PT Cruiser's smart interior, smooth ride, and unique retro style quickly attracted serious fans around the globe. They started PT Cruiser clubs and organized events. The PT Cruiser's design featured enough hot rod hints to attract the customizing crowd, too. Many mechanical artists saw the car as a **palette** for more chrome, more gadgets, and wild paint jobs.

Customizers proved that not all PT Cruisers are compact cars. Chauffeurs have fun driving the PT Cruiser stretch limousines.

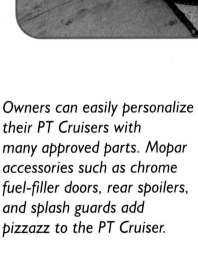

Owners can easily personalize their PT Cruisers with many approved parts. Mopar accessories such as chrome fuel-filler doors, rear spoilers, and splash guards add pizzazz to the PT Cruiser.

palette
    a blank surface on which artists mix colors

A fun "customizer" window lets fans create fantasy PT Cruisers on the car's official website.

The Specialty Equipment Manufacturers Association (SEMA) show puts the hottest, coolest, and most amazing custom cars on stage. PT Cruiser displays at SEMA have drawn gawkers of all ages.

Popular painted flames heat up the PT Cruisers hot rod styling.

Many PT Cruiser owners join clubs. In 2006, the retro band Sha-Na-Na sang about the PT Cruiser for hundreds of fans at the San Diego PT Cruiser Owners Club Rally.

PT Cruisers look primed for a trip to Victory Lane. Drag racing is especially popular. Many of these cars use modified racing engines. The cars must have roll bars and other safety equipment.

The Walter P. Chrysler Museum opened in 1999 on the DaimlerChrysler campus in Auburn Hills, Michigan. Its collection of cars, interactive displays, and car crazy gift shop attract visitors from around the world.

Many children use the PT Cruiser instead of Volkswagen Beetles for playing the back seat game of "slug bug." They say "Cruiser slug" instead of "slug bug."

Revved-up styling and modern performance shifted the PT Cruiser into the fast lane on the road to success. But the trip might be short. Some fans think this retro ride might be history by 2010. Whatever happens, the compact PT Cruiser has already earned a full-size legacy among car buffs.

Glossary

aerodynamics (ahr oh dih NAM iks) – engineering designs that allow air to flow easily over the body for greater speed

analog clock (AN uh log CLAHK) – a clock with hands

concept car (KAHN sept KAR) – a sample car used to try out designs and techniques

options (AHP shunz) – items not included in the price; the buyer pays extra for them

palette (PAL it) – a blank surface on which artists mix colors

production car (proh DUK shun KAR) – the final model, ready for manufacture

retro (RET roh) – designed to recall something from the past, such as a car model

sedan (suh DAN) – a car that seats at least four adults, usually with two rows of seats

simulation (sim yu LAY shun) – an example or model of a certain situation used to test ideas and make improvements

suspension (sah SPEN shun) – in a vehicle, the system of shock absorbers, springs, and other parts between the wheel and frame designed to create a smooth ride and better control

turbocharger (TUR bo char jur) – a special fan turned by the engine's exhaust gases that works to pump more air into the cylinders and boost power output

wheelbase (WEEL bays) – the distance between the front and rear axles

wind tunnel (WIND TUN nul) – a tunnel where air blows at known speeds to test a car's aerodynamics

Further Reading

Ackerson, Robert. *PT Cruiser: The Book of Chrysler's Classic Design for a Modern Age*. Veloce, 2007.

Maurer, Tracy Nelson. *Full-Throttle: Beetle*. Rourke Publishing, 2007.

Zuehlke, Jeffrey. *Concept Cars*. Lerner Publications, 2007.

Websites

www.chryslerheritage.com/pg500.htm

www.chrysler.com

www.ptownersclub.com

Index

About the Author

Tracy Nelson Maurer writes nonfiction and fiction books for children, including more than 60 titles for Rourke Publishing LLC. Tracy lives with her husband Mike and two children near Minneapolis, Minnesota.